Thank you for your service

From Sword to Pen

by PETER ANDREW TORRUELLA

illustrated by ANGEL MARTINEZ

◆ FriesenPress

Suite 300 - 990 Fort St
Victoria, BC, V8V 3K2
Canada

www.friesenpress.com

Copyright © 2016 by Peter Andrew Torruella
First Edition — 2016

All rights reserved.

No part of this publication may be reproduced in any form, or by any means, electronic or mechanical, including photocopying, recording, or any information browsing, storage, or retrieval system, without permission in writing from FriesenPress.

ISBN
978-1-4602-9322-5 (Hardcover)
978-1-4602-9323-2 (Paperback)
978-1-4602-9324-9 (eBook)

1. POETRY, SUBJECTS & THEMES, DEATH, GRIEF, LOSS

Distributed to the trade by The Ingram Book Company

TABLE OF CONTENTS

The Army And Liberty	1
Unnatural Selection	3
Life	5
Inviting Death	7
Step Right Up	9
Destruction	11
Look, Listen And Speak	13
Going Nowhere	15
Soldier On	17
Are You Going My Way?	19
What We Say	21
The Song	23
Burned	25
Betrayal	27
Blindfolded	29
No Vacancy	31
I Don't Love You Anymore	33
Dead Ends	35
Silent Darkness	37
Solitude	39
All Boxed Up	41
Battle	43
The Things I Want	45
My Dream Lover	47
In Plain Sight	49
No Need To Crawl	51
Changes	53

Effect Of Nature	55
Lost In Your Eyes	57
Need To Know	59
Inner Self	61
A Sneak Peak	63
Fly No More	65
Passion Found	67
True Love	69
A Child's Prayer	71
My Angelic Child	73
Reality	75
PTSD	77
Dream State	79
Sleep	81
Not Enough Time	83
Death	85
Change	87
Generations	89
Intestinal Fortitude	91
About the Author	93

Dedicated to all who suffer from PTSD
and their family and friends.

THE ARMY AND LIBERTY

The spirit of Liberty stands side
by side with the proud men and women

    of the Army

With her bright torch leading the way, Lady Liberty goes proudly with
the brave men and women

    of the Army

We bow our heads for the lost twin sons of Liberty
as their honor is carried in the hearts
of the proud men and women

    of the Army

With her light to guide us, we will unmask
the darkness that dampened the eyes
of the proud men and women

    of the Army

No more will we tolerate or negotiate the darkness!
The light of Freedom and Democracy will shine
ever brighter as Lady Liberty marches on
with the proud men and woman

    of the United States Army

UNNATURAL SELECTION

The sun, as it gracefully rises
The moon, as it gives its meaningful stare

    the twilight
    the twinkle
    the stars as they glare

The butterfly, silently heading towards death
The life of the land, inhaling its breath

then ... there is man

    with the power
    of life and death
    in the palm of his hand

Peter Andrew Torruella

LIFE

The toll is often paid by the ones who have

        the most

        to lose

Peter Andrew Torruella

INVITING DEATH

The shadow of death hovers over its prey awaiting the chance to take you away; it will carry you off to worlds far and wide where there's doom and disaster with no place to hide

A knock at the door is all that you'll hear; a cold chilling noise to warn you he's near; so if you are willing to take such a chance, keep up what you're doing and give death his dance

STEP RIGHT UP

step right up,
    come on in, it's time
for the circus to
    begin; don't worry
about that blood
    on the floor, you put
it there, been here
    before, I keep on
giving the love in
    my heart, you take
out a knife and tear
    me apart; one of
these days I'll lock my
    door, keep you from
spilling my blood on
    the floor; but for
now, come right in, it's
    time for the circus
to begin

Peter Andrew Torruella

DESTRUCTION

The moon is raising havoc upon the desert sand
The sun is nigh but there's no light upon the land

> your hopes are lost
> your dreams collide
> your fate is yet unknown

Knocking at your memories, you find that
no one's home; a twist of fate arises

> you see a lonely rose
> your fingers grasp it by the stem
> you pull it to your nose

you breathe in deep and fast but the scent is death and grime, for when you killed that little rose

> your life was lost in time

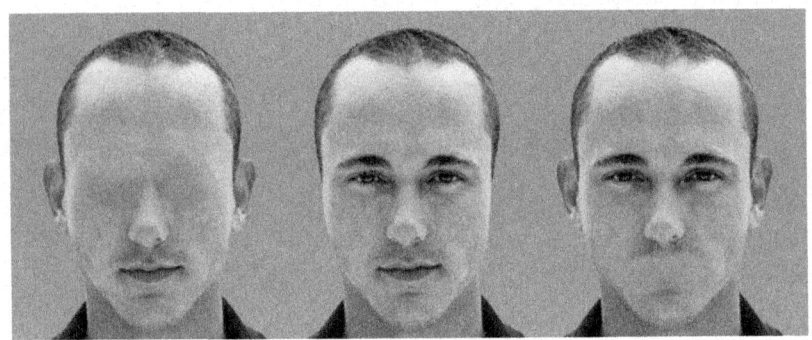

LOOK, LISTEN AND SPEAK

A man without sight can say:
    one does not need eyes to see beauty

A man who cannot hear can say:
    one does not need ears to listen

A man who is mute can say:
    one does not need words to say "I love"

A man without a heart can say:

  nothing

      nothing at all

GOING NOWHERE

Traveling everywhere
here and   there
going places that

      aren't

  any
      where

Meeting new people—I can see through
their disguises as they tell me stories
of love that turn out to be

      lies

SOLDIER ON

the smell of gunpowder,
the taste of blood once me,
smoke-filled eyesight, it's all I see

    soldier on, *dammit*, soldier on

someone I once knew, I can't recall
his name, lies in lifeless form;
I will never be the same

    soldier on, *dammit*, soldier on

go back home, they said to me, and
learn to love again; hard to do, when
I can't recall the name of my dear old friend

    soldier on, *dammit*, soldier on

ARE YOU GOING MY WAY?

    evil thoughts
        the twisted kind
        leave a soul without

    direction
    killer eyes play
        their part where love
        has no affection

    little kids leave
    books behind
        and shuffle off
        to school, while

    brainless thoughts
    corrupt the mind
        of unsuspecting
        fools

    so hop aboard
    the trip is free
        and ask yourself
        today

    are you ready to go with me
    are you going ... my way?

WHAT WE SAY

Oh, you poor child
so lonely, so cold
sitting in the light
so young, but so old

not knowing the true meaning
of the words that you've said
that rushed past your lips,
not from heart, but from head

never to be taken back
when words and ears they meet
the sadness you are feeling
the words so incomplete

these words we use the wrong way
on each and every day;
please, never say "I love you"
if you don't feel that way

 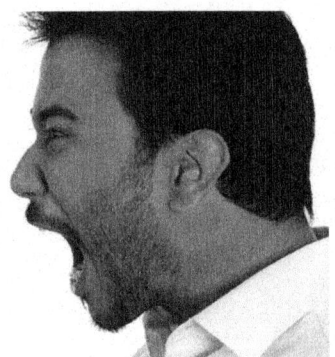

THE SONG

When I see you standing there, I want to run my
fingers through your hair, but when I look into your
eyes, I start to realize, you're looking right through

my soul

It's not enough for you to know how much I care—it's
just about fingers running through hair—and when I
look into your eyes, it's now I start to realize

it's not me
it's you that's not there

Now when you see me standing there, you'll think
about my fingers, your hair, and when you're looking
in my eyes, maybe you'll start to realize, I'm looking right through

your soul

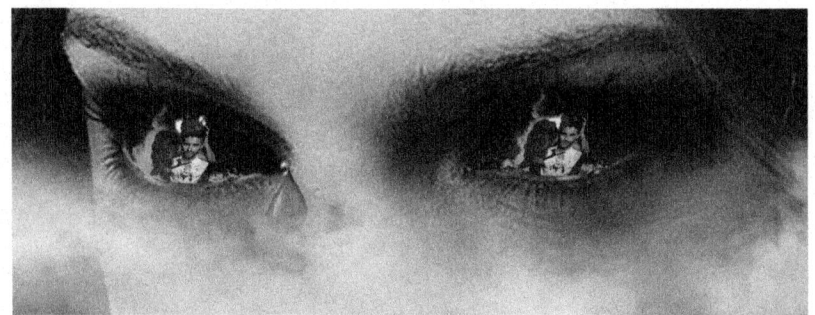

BURNED

    deep purple
    passions of a dark
    and lonely
    dream; dark
    and lustful
    memories
    that aren't
    what they
    seem; midnight
    stalking lovers
    take you
    to your cell
    while chanting
    spells of

passion

    and
    calling
    down
    to
    hell

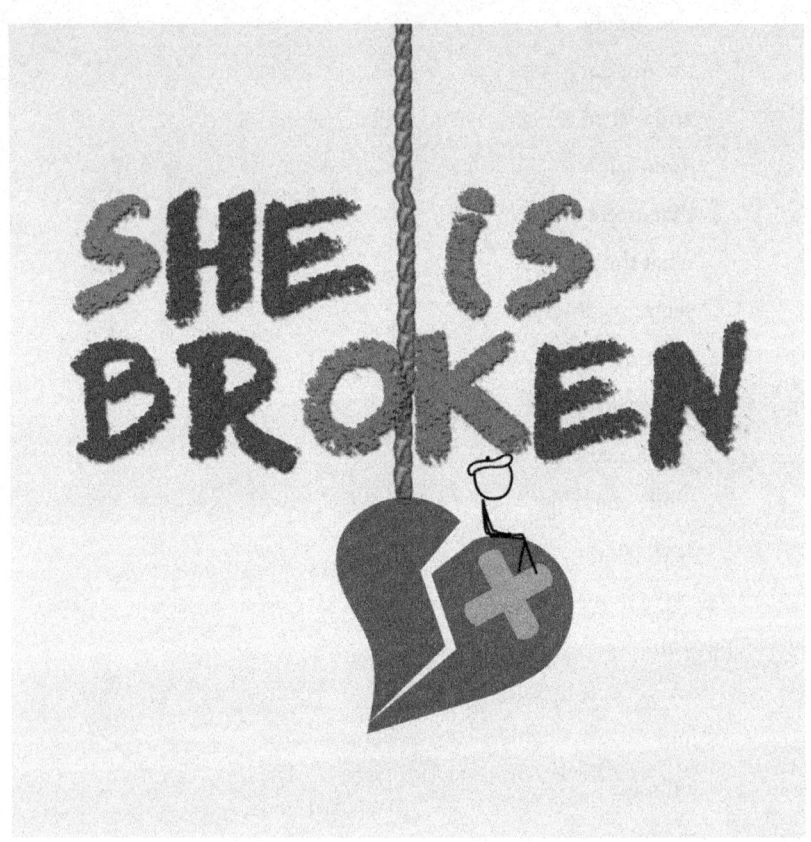

BETRAYAL

Being without you, knowing you don't care, what
am I to do when I wake and you're not there?

The battle lines are drawn, guns at the ready as
I wait till dawn, my aim tired, but steady

I will fight for you until I die or have you in my arms;
with dying breath I will try to hold your naked charms, but you insist
that Life is Good

without me by your side; you can't admit
like you should–

you took me for a ride

Peter Andrew Torruella

BLINDFOLDED

    I hide my eyes from you

                every time I lie

    I turn a deaf ear

                when I hear you cry

        I wait until you're sleeping before I
        crawl in bed with visions of another
        still trapped inside my head

    And no … I'll never leave you

        I'll stay and suck you dry and listen
        for the moment when I can hear

                you cry

NO VACANCY

How dare you knock on my door!

    I told you times before:

There's no room for you at my table

    you are an enigma
    (to say the least)
    not man nor beast

There's no room for you at my table

    from the darkness, were you born
    to fill the world with scorn

There's no room for you at my table

    for the last time I will say, you may hiss
    but slither away

There's no room for you at my table

I DON'T LOVE YOU ANYMORE

    I don't
    love you—get it through your head—it's
    all the things you do when I'm alone in bed

I don't love you anymore

    I tried
    my best to do what's right but—like the rest—
    you're not home at night

I don't love you anymore

    someone new
    with me tonight—she's right here by my side—so
    as I reach, turn off the light and kiss my brand new bride, I take a
    deep breath and say:

"I don't love you anymore"

DEAD ENDS

I've been looking around and the only place
I find me

       is in the mirror

              Dead ends, Dead ends

Where do I fit in? so tired of looking at myself
with my own eyes. All I see is what I am,
I can't see

       who I could be

              Dead ends, Dead ends

Where's the green light? I'll tell you where. Right in the middle of a

       four-way stop sign

              Dead ends, Dead ends

And me, approaching from all four directions. Who do I let go first?

       ... me ...

              Dead ends, Dead ends

SILENT DARKNESS

All alone

    I sit in my silent

        darkness

            Thoughts

                of how life use to be

        icy hands
        caress my soul, claiming all

      that once was me

Nevermore

      to feel tears
      upon my face

          icy hands
          of my darkness

              now fill that empty space

                  Silent darkness
                  is all that's left of me

SOLITUDE

ripples on the water
who's disturbing me?

this is my place of peace
not for all to see

I found this place long ago
it's just meant for one

my own self-made prison
I know what I have done

this place is my fig leaf
alone I bear this shame

no more pointing fingers
no one else to blame

do not try to break me out
just, please, leave me alone

ripples on the water
even though there's no one home

Peter Andrew Torruella

ALL BOXED UP

The lights are getting dimmer, the flaps are coming down, voices I once heard are now a muffled sound; the inner me that I once knew, not readily at hand, for in my haste to get away I left it in the sand and violent thoughts of pending doom now racing through my mind, I cannot find the real me that I have left behind; the drugs the doctors gave me were meant to calm me

down

Zombie in the living room

Zombie on the ground

BATTLE

        Unlike love

    hate lasts longer
but unlike hate

      Love can grow Stronger

Peter Andrew Torruella

THE THINGS I WANT

The chill of winter
on a hot summer day

The smile from a baby
that won't fade away

To mute the sound of hatred
from words that break my heart

A true love ever growing
that will not fall apart

MY DREAM LOVER

I have always known you, but
    only in my dreams
I hate to wake without you; don't know
    what this all means

                Is it my dreams that are true?
                Or that I can't stand being
                without you?

I can smell your perfume in the air as I lie
    awake at night
It's only when I go to sleep I have you
    in my sight

                I've never known you ... but I
                know you're there from the gentle whispery
                touch that shows you really care

Although we've never met, I know that
    you are real
Never will I forget the way you make
    me feel

                So if it's just a dream that makes me feel this
                way; never wake me from my sleep—I'll live
                my life
                this way

Peter Andrew Torruella

IN PLAIN SIGHT

I picked you up when you fell
Held open the door at the closing bell

Made you laugh when you were down
Helped to turn your frown around

Wiped the teardrops from your face
When you were ill I took your place

Gave you a chair so you could sit
Urged you on so you wouldn't quit

and still ... you don't know who I am

CHANGES

The beauty of a leaf slowly

        falling to

        the ground

        with its

        winter

        adornment

        is but a moment in time

        leaving us with ageless

        memories

Peter Andrew Torruella

EFFECT OF NATURE

As
the
wind
blows
through
the
flowers
and
trees
I can
taste
the
scent
of wildlife
as it
lingers
in my
body
and
makes
me
feel

invincible

LOST IN YOUR EYES

Never been here before
Never seen this place
Last thing I remember
I was looking at your face

Beauty all around me
Angels start to dance
Music playing tunefully
Puts me in a trance

I want to stay forever
But I know I can't remain
I must return to you
And hold you once again

But, how can I find you?
And then I realize
I was never far away
Just lost in your eyes

NEED TO KNOW

If I love you today
    will you love me tomorrow?
If I'm feeling lost and lonely
    will you understand my sorrow?

Will you turn down the path
    and decide to walk my way?
Will you gaze into my eyes
    without turning away?

Will you open your heart
    and respond to my plea
To reach out for my hand and
    share your love with me?

INNER SELF

Better to have never

drawn life's breath

than to have never

known the true essence

of her beautiful nature

A SNEAK PEAK

I dared to open my eyes
    when she gave her kiss to me
and to my great surprise
    an angel did I see

Locked in love, a tight embrace
    a frozen moment in time
her sweet breath upon my cheek
    told me she was mine

I will never let her know
    what I saw and felt that day
I want to let that moment grow
    and remember it just that way

FLY NO MORE

Oh, if it were so

    that I be winged upon an updraft to your
    heart to be then perched in the nest of your love

                              to fly no more

PASSION FOUND

In this world of hate and greed
I find that there's a real need
to let love into my heart

And since my passions have been freed
now to you I will concede
I have loved you from the start

Peter Andrew Torruella

TRUE LOVE

    As the tides
of the eternal
ocean gently
  unfold their
    cold-rippled
      waves onto the hot
  and crisp ever-vibrant
sun-soaked seashore,
the birds of this ocean
  gallantly proclaim
    the triumph
    of life and love.

As does my
heart, with its
  burning threshold
    of love and pounding
    necessity to give
  to you the virgin love
contained within
it and the life
  of its soul …
    forevermore

A CHILD'S PRAYER

Just before I lay me down, my knees
I place upon the ground
        My elbows rest upon the bed
        My hands support my weary head

And then I gather all my love, and pray
to our Lord God above
        For when he speaks, my heart
        does race; his love, I feel
        caress my face

No, I'm not perfect, yet, I win.
        When prayers and faith
        let God come in.

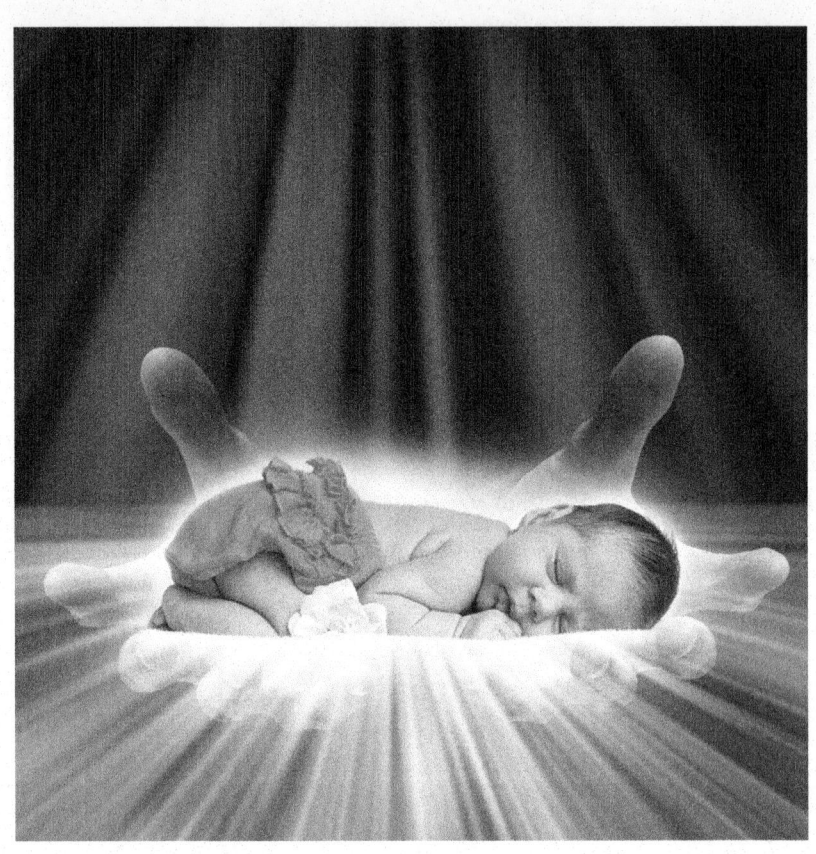

MY ANGELIC CHILD

As I turn the nightlight on
I look upon her face

in her dreaming moment
she lies there full of grace

I thank the Lord above
for what he's given me

a child born of love
for all the world to see

Peter Andrew Torruella

REALITY

    Unlike lightning

        fear finds its mark more than once

PTSD

Hairs on the back of my neck stand up as if called to attention—
feelings of utter doom enter my mind as I try to assess the current
situation—a threat awaits me—sight unseen—I get out of bed—and
let out a yell as I step on one of my kids' toys—cursing it all before I fall

A tired and groggy voice attempts to
come to my aid:

    "Are you alright honey!
        "Was it a dream?
            "… Are you afraid?"

                The voice has brought me back home and as I cry and
                rub my head, I murmur:

    "it will be ok sweetheart …
"just help me back to bed"

DREAM STATE

In the morning when I wake,
my dreams just wander by
then go back into dreamland
where people

       never cry
       never laugh
       nor sing
       nor joke

and ever would they say:
"who cares about emotions now …
tomorrow's … another day"

Yet, there are people in this world
who act the very same

       I just wish

that they would leave
exactly how they came

SLEEP

    Oh darkness, my old friend,

        so glad to have you here to take away my pain and brush
        aside my fear; the time I spend without you is painful and
        unreal; it's

        very hard to cope with the way life makes me
        feel; when I find it hard to cope with what life offers me, I close
        my eyes and drift away

        until you set me free; sleep, oh my sweet sleep,
        you also come for me, you bring to me the darkness and
        dreams that

                              set me free

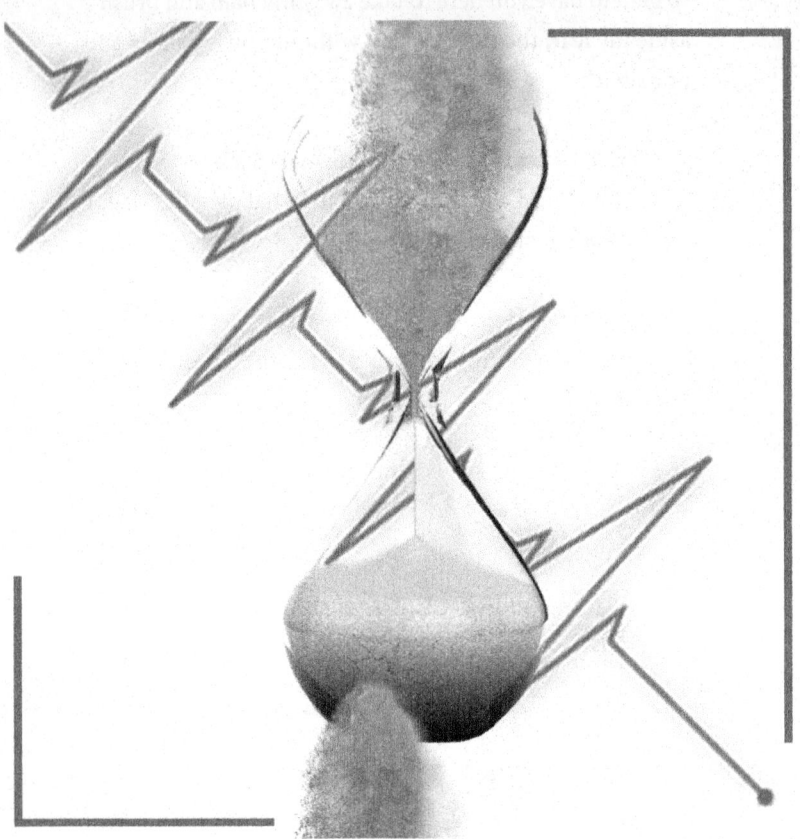

NOT ENOUGH TIME

If I had the time to tell you how much
I love you

I would still need to borrow more

DEATH

A form of sadness
we feel a sense of grief

on the verge of madness
our mind cries for relief

We get down on our hands and knees
and pray to God above

and ask him why he took away
the ones that we did love—

But then a calming fills your heart
and carries off your fear

For though you may be far apart
the love is very near

CHANGE

Long ago, in my distant past, I was a rough and tough guy; I never backed down from a fight; I always mixed truth with a lie—

>quick with my temper and fists; no care for my words that caused pain; no one I loved in my life; no reason for me to refrain

I'm no longer what I was in the past—

>no longer a rough and tough guy; try my best not to fight; never mix truth with a lie; slow with my temper and fists; care if my words will cause pain, because now with my son

>in my life

I'll never be that way again

GENERATIONS

　　　　when we are small

　　　we learn to walk, and after that we learn
　　　to talk, taught by what we hear from ones
　　　that we hold dear

　　　　and everything

　　　we hear said is carried off with us
　　　to bed and we will dream
　　　of what we heard and so remember

　　　　every word

　　　when we grow, we will teach
　　　the walk and after that we'll teach
　　　the talk and have ones

　　　　to send to bed

　　　we will know they dream of what
　　　we said; but they won't learn
　　　from just one word, for we will teach

　　　　them what we heard

INTESTINAL FORTITUDE

Unchallenged,
      we are but mere peasants

When challenged,
      we rise and surpass our

Greatest
      Expectations

ABOUT THE AUTHOR

Peter Andrew Torruella enlisted in the United States Army on August 5, 1980. For over 20 years, he served his country in multiple duty stations and deployments. On January 23, 2012, Torruella was medically discharged due to injuries suffered in combat, including post-traumatic stress disorder. The daily routine of dealing with PTSD is a hardship on himself, his family and friends. He hopes sharing his experience through poetry will help give people better awareness of the PTSD condition.